I Love You

Love Yourself
and Love Others
for a Fulfilling Life

DONNA HANKS

BALBOA.
PRESS

A DIVISION OF HAY HOUSE

Balboa Press books may be ordered through booksellers or by contacting:

Balboa Press
A Division of Hay House
1663 Liberty Drive
Bloomington, IN 47403
www.balboapress.com.au
1 (877) 407-4847

Because of the dynamic nature of the Internet, any web addresses or
links contained in this book may have changed since publication and
may no longer be valid. The views expressed in this work are solely those
of the author and do not necessarily reflect the views of the publisher,
and the publisher hereby disclaims any responsibility for them.

The author of this book does not dispense medical advice or prescribe the use
of any technique as a form of treatment for physical, emotional, or medical
problems without the advice of a physician, either directly or indirectly. The
intent of the author is only to offer information of a general nature to help
you in your quest for emotional and spiritual well-being. In the event you use
any of the information in this book for yourself, which is your constitutional
right, the author and the publisher assume no responsibility for your actions.

Any people depicted in stock imagery provided by Thinkstock are
models, and such images are being used for illustrative purposes only.
Certain stock imagery © Thinkstock.

Print information available on the last page.

ISBN: 978-1-4525-3175-5 (sc)
ISBN: 978-1-4525-3176-2 (e)

Balboa Press rev. date: 11/19/2015

To Mum and Dad

For your unconditional love and support,
I love you

"To thine own self be true"
William Shakespeare

Thank you, D.P.B., for reminding me of this.

Testimonials

"Donna, your book is fabulous!
Wise words and very elegantly expressed.
I love the cover!
Well done."

Siimon Reynolds
Advertising and business expert
Los Angeles

Readers' comments:

"Thank you for your book, I Love You. It helped to explain so many things to me; why I feel the way I do, and how to change these feelings. I now feel differently about my past and now know how to have a happier future. I was moved to tears."

— *D.C.*

"Wow! Now where was this book twenty years ago? Reading it has put so many things into perspective and given me some great tools to make a change, starting today. Everyone could benefit so much from spending some time with this book. Thanks a million for making change so achievable. I'm looking forward to a new beginning. This is the perfect book for my daughters to have on their e-readers. Love it!"

— *C.C.*

"A great book to remind us to get back to the simple things, enjoy our lives and value ourselves."

— *J. Y.*

CONTENTS

About the Author

At the age of eighteen, Donna Hanks read a poster in the staffroom of the *Kalgoorlie Miner*, the local newspaper she worked for in her hometown in Western Australia. "Change your thoughts and you change your world" was the quote by Norman Vincent Peale. Since then, Donna has taken a passionate interest in self-development, the power of the mind, and how to live your best possible life.

Donna continued to work in the advertising and media industries for ten years and loved it. Since 2001, she has been self-employed and has enjoyed many roles, including public relations, events, and talent management.

In 2011, Donna decided it was time to make a career from her passion: self-development. She began writing her book *Feel Good Now* and has since held numerous seminars and private coaching consultations, teaching others her theories on how to make positive change.

A Note from the Author

I have studied the subject of self-development and the power of the mind for more than twenty-five years. I don't have a formal qualification as such (i.e., no letters after my name), though I do like the sound of "Doctor Donna," so I may want to study to acquire a PhD at some stage. For now, I am happy to have life experience as my qualification.

At the time of publishing this book, this is how I describe my life: I share my life with my loving family, and they are my greatest joy in life. I see my close friends regularly; we talk, laugh, and travel together. I plan my own day, and I am doing what I love to do. I enjoy good health and feel totally grateful for all the good I have in my life and for my healthy family. I am also a work in progress. I believe that we all are. Some people say that those who teach self-development need to work on their own issues. I do agree that we "teach best what we most need to learn." This is why I love helping others; it motivates me to do as I suggest they do. Since focusing on loving myself, loving others, and following my own advice, I am definitely more fulfilled. I have ambitions and desires, though I am more relaxed about them since working on myself with the methods I'll explain in my books.

While reading about my theories, I invite you to relate this book to what *you* want from *your* life. I use examples from my own life to illustrate the points I make, but always be thinking about what *you* want when you read these examples.

This book is intended to be a summary; to help people who feel they want more from their life. My theories are what I believe in, developed from my experience to date. Those who have read this book have said that it has helped them to understand life situations better and helped them to change for the better. This is my aim: to help people feel good, live fulfilling lives, and love themselves. I ask you to start loving yourself now. If you love this book, give it as a gift to someone else who needs it.

I will donate 10 percent from every book sale to charities.

Thank you and I love you,

Donna

INTRODUCTION

This little book, *I Love You*, has finally come to fruition. It has taken a few directions and is now as it is meant to be. My gorgeous five-year-old son stated, as I was typing up these last words, "It is what it is." Now how is that for wisdom?

I have deliberated over some of the content; some say my writing and teaching style can be blunt, but I say sometimes it needs to be.

To quote the famous line by Eleanor Roosevelt, "Do what you feel in your heart to be right—for you'll be criticized anyway." Although I don't desire criticism (but it could be the risk I take for voicing my theories), I do feel in my heart that I needed to write and share my message.

I will follow that quote up with another one of my favorite quotes by the brilliant Dr. Seuss, "Be who you are and say what you feel, because those who mind don't matter, and those who matter don't mind."

I agree that you can't please all the people all the time. Understanding that not everyone is my reader, nor is everyone my fan, I want to help those who want to be helped and who like my ideas.

So after careful consideration and consultation with a few people regarding the content, I took a deep breath and wrote just what I wanted to say. One of my core messages is to be yourself, to be you, to be loving and caring, and to be true to yourself. Therefore, I write to you my thoughts and ideas for a fulfilling life, as I see it.

While writing my book *Feel Good Now*, which is full of practical and mindset techniques to live a fulfilling life, I decided I wanted to get the self-love message out in its own book.

I Love You is an introduction to my beliefs about making positive change, and it begins with self-love.

I believe loving yourself is the key to a happy and healthy life. In the bigger picture, my philosophy is that you can have anything you want, you can change anything you want, and you can create anything you want.

I believe that what you have in your life now is what you believe on a subconscious level. I teach how to change your beliefs on a subconscious level and how to take the actions to create the new beliefs and bring your desires into your reality. Start by imagining that you can have what you want.

I believe that we choose our thoughts, feelings, and actions. Think about this. If this is true, it gives us the power to think, feel, and act any way we like. This belief then empowers us to believe that we can have any thought or feeling we desire. Our thoughts and feelings determine our actions. That's a very empowering belief to start with.

The opposite of this belief is feeling like a victim. This belief is blaming others for your situation and feelings. If you want a happier and healthier life, I implore you to change this victim thinking now.

The new belief that you are in control of your own life creates a much happier place to be in. You can then go about changing anything you want. I choose to believe that we can change in any given moment and that change can be easy. So many people say it's hard. Why choose to believe anything can be hard when it can be easy? I understand that the changes required can be challenging (that's a better word to use than "hard"), but the decision to change is easy. Once the decision is made, and when you really mean it, the actions you need to take to get there *are* then easier.

If something in your life is not working for you, you can get different results by different thinking, feelings, and actions. If you agree with me that you choose your thoughts, feelings, and actions, then you have the power to change anything. This is a very powerful belief. Now is the time to take responsibility and make the changes.

If this belief is too much of a stretch from your current thinking, then read on and begin with this book, *I Love You*. Take steps toward your self-development. Ease into it if you need to. Some people don't want to change, and that's okay too. If you do want to change anything, and you want to learn a new way of thinking, then you're in the right place at the right time.

Your change or changes can be small, or you could need a complete overhaul. I can help you to change—if you want to change.

I don't know the emotional state or the life circumstances of every reader. I don't know *your* life story. Therefore, please take from this book what you can that relates to your own life and what can help you change it for the better.

If you require more information or need advice for further coaching, please visit my website, www.donnahanks.com

Thank You, Louise Hay

I needed to write this note to Louise, and my readers, before publishing this edition of *I Love You*.

I originally self-published *I Love You* as an e-book in June 2013. I did some self-promotion, to my friends via social media, and sold fifty e-books. I didn't have the strong drive to promote it extensively at the time. Perhaps I was waiting for the perfect timing.

I then experienced what I describe as a personal crisis. I did not feel I could teach others, as I was healing myself, physically and emotionally.

During this time, I was unpacking a box I hadn't unpacked for many years. I discovered my original copy of *You Can Heal Your Life* by Louise Hay.

Louise Hay was one of my original teachers when I discovered self-development and self-healing. Louise pioneered study of the mind-body connection, and she is a true mentor for me.

I flicked through a few pages of her life-changing book and was alarmed at how similar some of the content in my own book was to Louise's. As you'll read in the first chapter of *I Love You*, I talk about the importance of self-love and looking at yourself in the mirror to express and feel this.

Louise also teaches mirror work. I may have first learned this from her. I have learned many profound messages from Louise Hay.

I want to acknowledge Louise as one of my self-development teachers and as someone who has assisted me on my quest for self-healing.

I have learned from many others, namely Anthony Robbins, Siimon Reynolds, Abraham-Hicks, Dr. Wayne Dyer, and too many more to list.

In my search for answers and healing, I discovered the profound importance of self-love.

Since writing *I Love You*, I discovered other gems—similarities between Louise Hay and myself, in our writing and our life experiences.

I'll share a lovely story.

When I was in the process of writing and editing the first edition of this book, working from home and regularly printing out the book at the local printers, I'd excitedly bring it home and read it and edit it with red pen.

When it was finished, I proclaimed to my sons, "I have a book!"

My elder son replied, "It's not a book, it's a pamphlet."

It began as only sixty pages and has progressed to not many more pages. My intention was always to have a concise book.

I laughed at my son's comment and agreed that indeed it did look more like a pamphlet than a book.

Now, two years later, in 2015, after I discovered Balboa Press, a division of Hay House Publishing, and I decided to self-publish with them, I saw that Louise Hay tells a story in a video on the Balboa website. She tells of how her first teacher said her famous book, *You Can Heal Your Life*, was a pamphlet!

I took this is a sure sign that it was time to publish *I Love You*.

It does not matter whether it is a book or a pamphlet. I want to share my story and help others.

When I returned to revise *I Love You* (the edition you are reading now), I decided not to change the content.

From the time I first wrote *I Love You* to this publication, I had two more wonderful years of experience. My views had certainly changed in some ways, and I felt different.

I felt more like myself, the true me.

This only enhanced my message of the importance of self-love.

Thank you, Louise Hay, for the introduction to the idea of self-love, the power of affirmations, the mind-body connection, and for the opportunity to publish with Balboa Press.

CHAPTER ONE

Love Yourself Now

Do you love yourself?

What is the first answer that pops into your head?

If you're not sure, I'll explain my definition of loving yourself.

Loving yourself is liking who you are. Loving yourself is thinking and believing that you're a good person. It's having good thoughts about yourself. You love yourself inside and out; you love your mind, your personality, your thoughts, how you feel; you love your body and overall image. You feel good about yourself. You appreciate yourself.

Loving yourself is respecting yourself. I've heard it said that we want to be respected more than we want to be liked. Respect yourself first, by treating yourself as you want to be treated. When you love and respect yourself, you expect it from others, and you treat them with love and respect.

Loving yourself is accepting yourself as you are, approving of yourself, treating yourself with care, and having good habits. Good habits start with thinking good thoughts.

What you think about most of the time determines how you feel and how you act.

Your self-image is very important to your happiness. If you feel that you are not living your best life, if you are not acting and feeling in a way that is compatible with your self-image, this conflict can cause you to feel angry, frustrated, and unhappy, or worse.

As I aim to stay away from negative words and feelings, I want to show you how to love yourself and how to move toward positive emotions of feeling relaxed, happy, and fulfilled.

Be true to yourself. Who do *you* want to be? What do *you* want to do, and how do *you* want to feel? Ask yourself these questions, and answer them with all the honesty of your heart and gut feelings. If you're not sure how to answer any of my questions (or any question in everyday life), answer with your first thought, and listen to your intuition. What is your inner voice saying to you? Listen for the answers, as they are within you.

When people say they are looking for partners and not finding partners, I suggest that they focus on themselves—loving themselves and feeling good. I expand more on this subject in my book *Feel Good Now* when I explain the power of how your feelings create your reality.

For now, in the context of this chapter, make the changes you want to make in order to feel good about yourself, so that you send out a positive and appealing vibe. What qualities do you want in someone else? *Be* those qualities, to attract them. Start with yourself.

A positive self-image stems from feeling good about who you are, doing what makes you feel happy, and spending time with people who make you feel good. I believe that these are all important factors in feeling good and living a fulfilling life.

If you do love yourself, that's wonderful, and I'm sure you have a very happy life. If you don't love yourself, you're reading the perfect book for you right now.

In my experience, most people want to change something about themselves for the better.

> *The first step in creating the life you want is to love yourself now. Start with saying aloud, "I love myself now, as I am."*

Love every part of yourself, and if you want to change something, resolve now that you will do it. If you don't want to change it, accept it.

You can love yourself without thinking that you are perfect. I use the word "perfect" a lot in my writing and coaching, and I say it to mean that something is "perfect for you." I can feel perfect as I am right now, even though I still have things I want to change. And I can be working on changes while also loving myself.

Accept yourself as you are now. You need to accept yourself as you are now before you will be able to change—if you want to.

Love yourself now, and feel good about it. That's the key. I encourage you to think that you're okay as you are now. If you love and accept yourself now, as you are, that creates a good feeling. A good feeling will create more good feelings.

Think to yourself that you *can* change if you want to. You *can* do more, you *can* improve any area of your life (or all of it).

Loving yourself is allowing yourself to be your best.

***Think and believe now that you
can have your best life.***

Take a good look at yourself, inside and out. Look at yourself in the mirror for added effect. Bonus points for your self-development if you can do this naked. I call this the naked exam. It is like an exam: you are examining yourself. You're deciding what you want to keep and what you want to change. It can be challenging to strip naked and stare at yourself in the mirror and really accept yourself. I expect that this will be emotional. That is the point. When you get emotional about an issue, that provides the fuel that motivates you to change what you want changed.

You might do the naked exam and not want to change; you might instead just decide that's who you are and that you are wonderful.

Whichever result you experience, I want you to do the naked exam. It brings so many benefits. Your emotions could range from pure love to disdain for yourself. You could feel embarrassed when you look at yourself in the mirror. I know that some people can't do this. Some cringe to look at themselves. Others may feel that they just don't want to. But imagine how your life could change if you could do this exam and feel good about yourself. You could look at life differently because you would have more confidence. You could relax about the little details. You could laugh at yourself more. You could simply enjoy your life more. This could empower you to be your best.

My emotions and reactions when I look at myself naked have changed as I have become more self-assured. I'm sure they will for you too. I now feel relief that I can confidently look myself square in the eyes and say, "I love you"—and really mean it. Please try this. I'm sure you will reap many positive benefits from it. If you can't do it naked, start with an exam while clothed. But I strongly suggest that you work your way up to the naked exam.

Look at yourself in the mirror and say out loud, "I love you, (and say your name)." Mean it, and just "be" with yourself. Be alone. Laugh at yourself, if this works for you. Cry if you need to. Get all the emotions out. No one is watching you; this is for you. It will benefit your whole life, in my opinion.

If you want to, talk to a friend or partner about how you feel about yourself and the changes you want to make. You can prefer just to keep this to yourself. Feel the feelings you have about yourself, and only share them if you want to.

If you have really had enough of the status quo, that may be all the motivation you need to make positive changes. When you really have that feeling of "enough" or "never again," it can motivate you to change. This is the fuel I mentioned. There might be something about you physically or emotionally, or it could be the way you feel you are being treated.

I believe that we teach others how we want to be treated. Now is the time to regain control of your life, starting with your assessment of your own self-worth.

How you feel about yourself and how you treat yourself will determine how others treat you and what you attract in your life. It's all about the energy you radiate, and we'll talk more about this in forthcoming books.

Put this book down now and go and do the naked exam—or do it when you next have the opportunity to be alone.

> ***The good news is that you get to pass your own naked exam. You're the one who decides that you're amazing, worthy, and lovable.***

Notes

CHAPTER TWO

The Power of Praise

I believe that loving yourself is the key to excellent health, harmonious relationships—and anything else you desire. I want you to feel good about yourself and project this good feeling onto all around you.

A crucial element of loving yourself and others is the power of praise.

Positive self-talk is integral to loving yourself. Say and think to yourself when you've done something well: *I am good at that*; *I am an awesome parent*; *I am kind*; *I help people*; and any other positive statement you can think of.

I talk a lot about affirmations in this book and in coaching. Affirmations are very powerful, as they are positive statements, asserted in the present tense. The idea of an affirmation is to imprint this statement into your subconscious mind so that you believe it. Always state your affirmations in positive, present, tense, starting with the words "I am." If you feel that a firm statement is too drastic a change from your current thinking, you can use the words "I am improving" or "I am working on" to help your subconscious gradually believe the new message. One of these bridging words, such as "improving," can help to move you toward the new belief, rather than making a big jump.

Praise yourself and tell yourself how good you are. You can just think these statements if you don't want to say them aloud.

I talk aloud to myself all the time (yes, I get funny looks in shops). I've always done this. It works for me to tell myself when I've done a good job, and for me it comes easily. My parents have always bragged of my successes, so I have learned this behavior from them. If you need help with this, just start somewhere. You must know of something good about yourself. If you're feeling low, remember something at which you once excelled or any positive memory of feeling good about something you achieved. Focus on that to start with.

> *It's okay to boast about yourself, even if it is just to yourself. This message is still getting into your subconscious mind, and I believe the subconscious mind is running the show (your life).*

In contrast, I see so many people who tell themselves how bad, ugly, fat, or useless they are. I have seen and heard it so many times that it inspired me to write this and urge you to affirm what you want. I have been around people who have said "I feel fat" to themselves—and the people in the room can hear them. Along with these thoughts, these people have the body language to match: slumped shoulders, shuffling, looking down. This affirms their negative feeling. They receive the negative feeling in their minds and then act it out in their lives. I'll use common examples, and one common negative feeling is to not love your body shape and size.

My suggestion is to think about what you *do* want, (the positive feeling), and then say that and instill that into your mind.

Replace the negative thoughts with the positive: *I feel fat* becomes *I feel great* or *I am working on getting fit. I feel ugly* becomes *I feel good about myself,* or *I am working on feeling good about myself.*

Use words that feel good for you, but make sure they are positive and in the present tense. "I am" is a very powerful statement. You are making a statement to yourself. Think about this. You can be anything you want. So change your "I am" statements to what you want to be.

If this feels strange to you, (to affirm positive beliefs and tell yourself how good you are), if you feel that your life is mundane or that you don't have many good qualities, start with anything you can think of.

If you have children, love yourself for having the privilege of having them (remember, not everyone can have children). Love yourself for being a great parent. If you feel that you're not a great parent, love yourself for trying to be your best, and vow today that now you will be.

Positive talk, praise, and encouragement are vital for all children. I compliment and encourage my children constantly. I am always telling them: "You're clever"; "you're kind"; "you're so well-behaved"; "you're beautiful"; "I love you." I'm very enthusiastic; my compliments are gushing. I love to compliment and encourage my boys. I discipline them when it is needed, but there is more love, kindness, and compassion than any other emotion. I shower them with affection.

I urge them to encourage one another. If the older boy doesn't want to join in an activity the younger one is engaging in, I say, "Okay, if you don't want to stick googly eyes on a felt animal, just encourage him."

So my older son will sit down next to his brother and say, "Good job, buddy," and the younger one will beam with pride.

This is so simple. Encourage and praise yourself and others. I believe that it helps people to feel good about themselves and keep going.

It has been proven that you can learn any new skill, but you have to practice it (remember: practice makes perfect), so encourage anyone who says they want to do anything.

It only takes one person to encourage another for that person to turn his or her life around. Be the person who makes a difference—in your own and in someone else's life.

I compliment anyone who crosses my path, not just my kids. Once, I accidentally recorded myself for twenty minutes while I was shopping (I'd bumped the "record" button on my phone). When I played the video, watching myself from the perspective of the view from my jeans pocket, I was pleased and amused. "Hello, how are you?" ... "Love your nails" ... "Love your hair" ... "Love your dress." These were the comments I had given people I ran into while shopping. I hadn't met any of these people before. It was like a snapshot of my life, and I could see how enthusiastic I was when I complimented people.

I believe in giving to receive, and I love to receive compliments. The idea I want to impress upon you is to give freely. Please do what you can to spread happy vibes, so we all emanate positivity. If you're not already doing this, increase your encouragement and compliments to your friends and family, especially your own children. It creates more of the same. I believe in the power of praise. Praise your children, praise your friends and work colleagues, and praise yourself.

Notes

Chapter Three

Let Go of Judgment

When you truly love yourself, you don't need to judge others. You can try to help them, but you don't need to judge. Do you notice that the people who are always judging others don't seem happy with themselves? Notice the self-assured, happy people. You can tell by their energy. They are happy with themselves and they feel secure, so they don't need to judge others.

I understand that it can be challenging not to judge. I often don't understand why people do what they do, but in the same way, they may not like or understand my choices. It's best to leave people be, unless they want help, of course. I help people if they want to be helped. If they are happy doing what they're doing, then I let them be. I expect the same from others. Life experience has taught me this gem of wisdom.

My family made a big change in our lifestyle a few years ago, and many people thought it was okay to tell me that they didn't agree with it. That was when I decided not to judge others, as I didn't like the feeling of other people doing it to me. This decision was right at the time, and it was a personal choice.

If I think, *I wouldn't do that* (of other people's decisions), I just don't say it, unless the person asks my opinion. If someone asks your opinion or asks for your advice, that's when I think it's appropriate to give it. There is a big difference between giving an unwelcome and negative opinion, and lovingly helping someone in need. Remember that your tone and body language will always set the mood. Telling loved ones something they need to hear can be done in a loving way.

In my experience, most of us make comments about how others are living their lives. I believe that it's good to get things off your chest; tell a close friend or partner if you need to, then let it go and move on. I say it's good to vent; I talk to my friends and my family about what's bothering me. I feel so good after talking to someone. My mum is my best confidante. I feel good just being around my mum; she exudes kindness and love. She is so caring and loving and is an amazing listener.

I encourage others to seek counseling if they need to, from a loved one or a professional counselor. I think it's healthy for people to talk about their issues to someone loving and caring who will really listen. This is different from people projecting their woes onto everyone who crosses their path. I believe that, if someone keeps talking about and focusing on a problem, the constant attention amplifies it.

My advice is to talk about it, decide what you're going to do to change it, and then go about changing it. I see people who spend most of their time judging others. Take notice of how much you judge others. If you're doing it all the time, it drains your energy. Use this energy instead to fix yourself. Do something for yourself to improve your own life.

> **You will feel better when you stop judging others and focus on yourself.**

It is good to help others when they're in need. Help people when you can, without judgment.

Imagine what could happen if everyone stopped judging and instead used all this energy on loving. This could eliminate anger, bullying, and all types of violence and abuse. I believe that angry people and bullies don't like themselves. They take their anger out on other people who often aren't strong enough to defend themselves. I believe that, if you feel good about yourself, you don't need to push other people around.

If you are the one being bullied, stand up to the bully. They don't usually expect it, and this can sometimes be all it takes for them to retreat. If the bullying persists (whether at home by a partner, at school, or in the workplace), you need to do something about it. Don't allow yourself to be bullied anymore. If you don't know what to do, I suggest that you start by talking to someone about the issue. Tell someone loving and caring that you are being bullied. Ask for help, and believe that there will be someone to help you. Someone loving and caring will help you find the courage to leave an abusive situation—and this can relate to verbal abuse, not just physical abuse.

Talking about your feelings is the key if you are being bullied or if you are the bully. Men and boys can be conditioned to not talk about their feelings. Whether you are male or female, please believe that it is better to talk to someone and to fix the situation than to stay in a harmful situation because you are scared or too proud to admit the problem. I urge you to seek help if you are in a harmful or abusive situation.

If you are a parent, encourage your children to talk about their feelings.

Ideally, loving yourself and others prevents bullying in the first place. The next-best move is to help the bully. If you know a bully, (if not your child, is it your friend, your neighbor, colleague, or relative?), ask that person if you can help. You don't need to get any more involved than asking that question. Maybe no one has cared enough to ask before. You could change someone's life for the better, just by asking that person to talk about his or her problems.

Notes

CHAPTER FOUR

Love Your Children

Start with loving yourself, and build up your self-esteem if it is lacking. Love yourself, and love your children.

For many reasons, we need to show and tell our children that we love them, that they are worthy of love, that they are lovable. We need to show them how to treat others with love, kindness, and respect.

Be careful how you speak to everyone, especially children. I believe that positive talk to your own children begins when they are *in utero*—before they are born.

If you believe that an unborn child can pick up on your energy and feelings, then remember this if you are pregnant or if you know someone who is pregnant. Think about what you say in her presence. If you or your partner is pregnant, tell your unborn child how much you love him or her and that you can't wait to meet him or her.

Really feel love for your child (at all times), and the child will feel it and know it—and that child will learn to be loving to others.

Children need to feel loved. Everyone needs to feel loved. Be loving to yourself and be loving to others.

Do what you can to feel good for yourself and for others.

I agree with the theory that beliefs are formed in early childhood, when we receive messages—whether spoken or unspoken—from others. A belief can be formed from a look, and such a look can have an effect even if it is from someone we don't know. A belief can be formed after hearing something only once. I had a very happy childhood, and my parents and others loved and encouraged me. I also have beliefs formed from what they and others have told me during my life. You can choose to change these beliefs, with your positive self-talk and affirmations.

It can take people many years of unhealthy relationships and experiences and years of counseling to work on their issues and undo the bad feelings. My message to you is that it doesn't have to take years to undo the bad feelings. You may have some work to do on yourself, but the sooner you start, the better. Make sure to spend as much of your time as possible around those who support your new beliefs about yourself, those who aren't keeping you in the "old place."

I have two brothers (I'm in the middle), so I always felt special; I was the "princess" of the family. Mum and Dad would say, "And here's our little girl." I still feel special every time they "present" me. I have a very close family and have wonderful memories of growing up.

I remember that Mum and Dad did all they could to give us what we wanted. I remember having the material items we wanted, but more importantly I remember the loving feelings.

I love the saying about being present for your children, rather than giving them presents. I say it's okay to do both—but being there for them and being involved and loving is essential.

I remember feeling really loved, and I still do. This is my most dominant emotion from my family and childhood.

I feel safe with my family. I remember saying to my dad only a few years ago, "I feel safe with you." I'm not sure he knew what to say, but I'm sure he was pleased. My dad likes to protect me and my family. Now, this is a good feeling; it's one of those feelings that I will always remember. All the good feelings can overcome any less-than-desirable moments I may have had. Similarly, I feel safe with my husband, my mum and my two brothers. I have sought this feeling in my other relationships, and thus I attract people with whom I feel safe.

Because I like to feel safe (and, through childhood conditioning, I know how it feels), my strong instinct is to want to protect my own children.

What a lovely experience: to feel safe and loved. I want this for you too. Create a loving and safe environment for yourself and your children.

I believe that people create more of their most dominant emotions. So I ask people in coaching: What is your most dominant emotion? I then tell them that that is what they will get more of. *Feel Good Now* explains this in more detail, with a description of how people attract more of what they already have. Make sure your most dominant emotions are positive.

I believe that my loving childhood has led me to have a very positive self-image. However, those who have not had a loving childhood can still go on to achieve amazing results by working on the bad memories and creating new positive beliefs.

I think that memories are a person's own interpretation of events. It's how we create meaning from something. But your interpretation of an event can be different from someone else's. It's *your* interpretation of what you experienced.

When I think of my childhood, I remember the good and loving times, and the negative experiences are few or forgotten.

What you choose to focus on is integral to your happiness. Your focus is essentially your life. You'll feel, and react to, what you're focusing on.

My intent for you is to have a positive self-image now, regardless of your past, and your current beliefs.

> *We can't change our pasts, but we can change how we want to feel now—and thus create our new positive futures.*

It's not *just* your childhood that determines how you feel now. I believe that it's a big part of how you feel now, but your whole life experience contributes to how you'll feel throughout your life. For example, you can have a happy and loving childhood and then have a negative experience that changes your whole outlook. If you were once happy but an unpleasant event caused you to experience sadness or hopelessness, you can turn this around by deciding that you want more out of life and by applying the changes I suggest.

> *Regardless of your past and your interpretation of events, know that anyone (and that includes you) can change at any time and start living his or her best life.*

Choose not to dwell on the past but to focus on what you want to create for your future.

If you haven't had a loving family, you can create new beliefs for yourself, and you can help others by being loving to them.

If you haven't been around people who made you feel loved and safe, you can change that now. Think that you now want this—and, by doing so, attract these people.

If you have received unhealthy messages from others, you can change this by choosing new beliefs about yourself.

I have lost count of the stories I've heard of sisters (or brothers) where one is touted as the "good-looking one" or the "smart one." I know many people who do not feel good and have lost their self-worth, feeling that they are not as good as their siblings or that they're not pretty or smart enough.

Sometimes I meet children and the younger one stands out as particularly cute, but I always acknowledge the others. "Aren't you adorable, and so are you!" I say, and I'll be very conscious of including them all in my praise.

This is only one example of how we must do everything we can to love and support our children. Even if we don't feel well, if we are angry, depressed, or just not enjoying our life to the fullest, we should not let them see this. Children learn from the example you set. Let's be the good example we want them to copy. And—I urge you to seek help if you are feeling angry, depressed, or sad most of the time.

My quest to feel good began when I became a parent. I want to be the best I can be as a parent. But as every parent knows, during the day-to-day challenges of raising children it's possible to fall short of that ideal.

One day, after one too many outbursts at my children, I thought, *there has to be a better way.* So I consciously began changing whatever I could to feel more even-tempered, relaxed, and in control of situations. I wanted to be better for them—and for myself.

At that stage of my life, my angry moments were not that common (i.e., there were a lot more happy moments than angry ones), but there were still too many for my liking, and they were unnecessary. I took out my frustrations on the kids when I was tired or hormonal and, immediately after doing this, I had a feeling of deep regret. I felt regret that I had overreacted to the situation; this regret became the motivation to change my behavior. Then I stepped up my quest to feel good (with no angry outbursts), and the subsequent changes I've made, including in nutrition and exercise, have resulted in a calmer, more balanced, happier, and healthier me.

Do you want to be calm, kind, nurturing, and loving to your children and the people all around you? I certainly do. I do what I can to feel good—for myself and to all those around me. What I aim for as a parent is loving thoughts, feelings, actions, and good times most of the time. If I do have unpleasant moments, I want them to be minor and insignificant. So far, so good with this aim, as this style of parenting enriches my family.

"I love you" is the last thing I say to my boys when I say goodbye to them and put them to bed at night. I am very generous with saying, "I love you" to my sons, I tell them numerous times a day. I say "I love you" when signing off phone calls to my loved ones. These are the most important words you can say, I believe.

When my teen son says, "ILY" to me (acronym of I love you), it instantly lifts my mood. If he's being a testing teenager, he quickly chimes in a timely "ILY," and it instantly changes the mood to positive. It's as if he realized he was being unpleasant and knows the "magic words" will get a good response. With his change in words and my positive reaction, he also feels better. I still need to deal with the issue at hand (inappropriate behavior), but saying "I love you" can defuse and allow healing in any situation.

I love you. They really are magic words. Use them, and all around you will feel good. Back up these words with true feelings of love, and show you mean it by your actions.

I am very conscious of complimenting my children equally. I also like to spend time with them one-on-one, absolutely smothering them with love and attention. I often tell my children to think good thoughts. Now my youngest says this to me. If he sees that I am about to react to something that once would have upset me, he'll quickly say, "Think good thoughts, Mum."

Recently, I was talking to my boys about respecting one another and playing nicely (encouraging the opposite of being rough with one another). My younger son said to my older son, "I love you 100 percent." I was in awe of that prophetic statement and encouraged the older one to repeat it back. He did. Now that's love.

That sums up my message: Love yourself 100 percent. Love your children, friends, family, and partner 100 percent.

If you're a parent, I'm sure you'll agree that it is the most challenging and rewarding role you will ever have. It's also the biggest responsibility. Be your best for yourself so you can be your best for your children.

Even if you are not a parent, you can apply my theories to all your relationships. You can be more loving and encouraging to your work colleagues, partner, friends, and everyone you meet. You'll notice the difference in your mood—and your whole life—when you are kind and loving.

Notes

Chapter Five

The Impressionable Teen Years

I have many memories of how I formed beliefs, and there were quite a few from my teen years. This seems to be a very impressionable age. Teens look for approval, compare themselves to others, and want to know if they're good enough.

I remember asking my best friends, "Is she prettier than me?" when my ex-boyfriend had a new girlfriend.

My good friends responded with, "Of course not; you're better." But still I needed to ask.

As I refer to a few stories about how I look, I can see how easily people can be programmed to believe that our looks define us.

If you have received this message, that you are defined by your looks, you can now decide to love yourself, as you are now. Your looks do not need to define you. However, you will often be judged by the way you look. This is why I believe that it is important to love yourself.

> *Loving yourself trumps any thoughts that another may have about you, and how can you ever know how someone else really feels?*

Others can tell you how they feel, and they can show you how they feel by their actions, but you can only really know and believe how *you* feel.

Be happy as you are (or go about changing it), but always feel that you are doing your best. It is up to you to decide what and who you are now; that is how the world will see you. How you feel about yourself and how you treat yourself is how you will *be* treated.

> *You set the standards for your life.*

I can now see that if a man chooses another woman over me, it doesn't mean that she is prettier or that I am not pretty enough.

We often understand situations in hindsight and not when they happen. I want to help adolescents now, as well as anyone else who needs this lesson, by asking that people not compare themselves to others but to be their true selves.

31

If your beloved chooses someone else over you, I know how heartbreaking this can be (I've been there too), but console yourself with thinking that there is someone better for you.

You are pretty (or handsome) enough, good enough, clever enough, and you are truly lovable.

Be around people who also feel that you are good enough.

I have had the same three close girlfriends since childhood. One I met in the first grade and the other two when we were in high school. I have other dear and supportive friends who have also had an influence in my life, but my three friends from childhood are still my best friends. These are the friends I can rely on, the ones who'll tell me what I want to hear—and also tell me something I may not want to hear but that I need to know. These friends have been in and out of my life over the years, but we are all there for each other, and it is a very good feeling.

Spend time with the people who make you feel good; you know who they are.

Having close friendships creates a very special feeling. We all need people around us who will love and support us and be there when we need help. I believe that close friendships are integral to feeling good and having a fulfilling life.

Value and nurture all the positive relationships in your life. Your partner or romantic relationship is integral to how you feel about yourself, and this seems more obvious to us than the effect our friends and family have on us, but everyone we spend time with on a regular basis has an influence on us.

If you are not enjoying close friendships now, you can change this by *being* a good friend. Start acting in the way that you would like to be treated. If you want something, give it. If you want good friendships, do something nice and thoughtful for someone else. If you want more love in your life, *be* more loving.

> **Be sure to be around those who support you, love you, encourage you, and just let you be you.**

The special friendships formed in our teen years have so much influence on us, I believe. For me, it's like going back to the old friends whom I can rely on. This makes so much sense, as these are the friends who made us feel good about ourselves back in the day—when we were so unsure of ourselves. By reflecting on my own teenage years, I can see that the ages of thirteen and fourteen were integral to shaping my beliefs about myself. Teens in my day would seek approval from their friends in person and on the telephone, whereas now, social media have been added to the mix; nowadays, teens (and some adults) seek approval from how many "likes" they have.

The teen years are a vital time for parents to encourage their children to have a strong sense of self. Help them to be good people. Your children will look to you, the parent, for guidance, affection, and love. They need boundaries and discipline, but they also need love and attention. Tell your teenagers that they are good enough. Striving to be perfect can be an issue, so tell them they are perfect as they are.

My parents have always been loving, supportive, complimentary, and caring to me, and I particularly remember feeling close to them in my teen years. While we had strong boundaries and often had consequences for our bad behavior (being grounded from the party on the weekend was the utmost of punishments), I still recall mostly love and support from my parents and brothers.

I believe that we develop our identities during these crucial teenage years, and so I am particularly concerned with whom my own children spend time with. I see how happy they are when they are with people they feel they can be themselves with, when they're not trying to impress anyone. It's good to see this in anyone.

If you are a parent, do you know whom your children are spending time with on a regular basis? Keep an eye on this. Get to know your children's friends, especially if they are teens. You're the gatekeeper for their major influences, and the teen years are, I believe, a crucial stage in their lives. I ask a lot of questions to all kids who visit my house. Sometimes this is embarrassing for my teenage son, but he knows this is the way it is. I need to be happy with the people he is spending time with.

I am happy when he helps a friend in need. I couldn't be prouder than when I see my sons behaving lovingly and helping others. I love hearing that they have been well-behaved while visiting other people. Sure, we have the usual teen antics, but most of the time their behavior is good and loving.

Be kind to all around you, in person and on social media. We all know, from the vast amount of media attention, how disapproval and bullying on social media can be just as detrimental—if not worse—as it is in person. My aim is for you to be kinder to those around you, be kind to yourself, and reduce the negative messages.

While we're talking about the influential teen years, I'd like to share a little story about loving yourself.

I met one of my aforementioned best friends when we were fourteen. I will refer to her as my BBF. That's not a typo. BBF stands for beautiful best friend. By the way, my BBF may not like me referring to her in this way, but I need to say this to make my point. I'll call her BBF, as I thought she was beautiful and had lovely features I didn't have—long, thick, dark hair, alabaster skin, and a perfectly shaped small nose.

As a child and teenager, I had a less-than-desirable nose (it was flat and broad). I didn't think of myself as good-looking, perhaps cute at best. My nose did bother me at times, and I had my share of nicknames and teasing, but I would laugh with the hecklers. I remember this very meaningful conversation I had with my BBF, when we were fourteen.

Scene: We were both looking in the mirror, putting on makeup.

Me: I wish I had your nose.

BBF: I wish I had your legs.

That was the extent of that life-changing conversation.

I hadn't even thought of it until that moment: I had something that BBF thought desirable. I was thrilled that she envied something I had. That was the turning point for me to focus on my good parts—my legs—rather than my nose.

As an adult, I felt that my nose was less obvious. In later years, BBF had more pearls of wisdom.

"You seem to have grown into your nose," she said when we were older. Her sage opinion meant everything. Her acknowledgement of this was more approval that my nose was better. In recent years, another childhood friend asked me if I'd had a nose job. I haven't. I simply grew into my nose.

The moral of this story is to accept your perceived shortcomings. If it's a body part you feel you can't change, maybe you will grow into it. I've encouraged you to change the aspects of yourself that you want to change and focus on your good parts. Another important aspect of this story is the effect certain people have in your life and how their approval or disapproval can shape your thoughts—even about your nose!

Now, I still see BBF as beautiful, and I also love and appreciate her many other good qualities; she is funny, articulate, and a loving, devoted mother.

> *Often we need to look beyond how a person looks,*
> *and notice how we feel when we are with them.*

As an adult, I now feel very secure about my looks. I'm vain even, and I feel good this way. I know how to accentuate my good parts.

Deep down, it's all about how you feel about yourself. Getting compliments and approval from others is nice, but when you approve of yourself, it doesn't matter what others think. It's like the compliments are a bonus, as you already feel good.

I recall when I was a teenager, we would say, "She loves herself," referring to someone who was conceited. Maybe she was the girl who strutted around the schoolyard with utmost confidence. It was looked upon unfavorably to love yourself.

Loving yourself can sound like vanity, but I say it is okay to be vain. You can be vain and still be loving and caring. I certainly am.

Look at the person who appears to "love herself" in a new, positive light. Now, you do the same.

It is a really good feeling to truly love yourself.

Be you, and be happy being beautiful you.

Notes

CHAPTER SIX

Create New Beliefs

If you want to improve your self-image at any stage of your life, start with affirmations of positive new beliefs.

I believe that you can decide to change any belief. You can do this quickly, or it may take some time to get the new message into your subconscious. I think it depends on how serious you are about changing. If you try for today only and then go back to your old ways and thinking, then nothing will change. If you keep trying, and keep affirming, and keep taking different actions, you will get different results to back up your new beliefs. You can choose to change by choosing different thoughts and feelings and acting differently. You can make the decision quickly—how about now?

My suggestion for a new affirmation is:

I now believe that I can change how I feel about myself.

One simple example of a limiting belief is to think that you are clumsy. "Butterfingers" was the saying when I was younger, and if you were always told you were clumsy, you'd believe it and keep doing it. I used to drop things. I still drop things. Okay, so I'm the "butterfingers" in this story. I can decide now to say, *I am careful* and affirm the opposite of *I am clumsy*.

This belief seems harmless, and there are more serious negative beliefs to have, but you can use the same theory to change any of them. If your current belief is *I am always late*, change this to *I am always on time* or *I am always early*. If your current belief is that you are unattractive, you can change that now to believe that you are attractive. Affirm the opposite of your negative belief. You can make the decision now to have new beliefs about yourself; the sooner, the better. You can help others by giving them positive messages. They will then not have any negative belief to undo, at least not from you.

If we all do this, it eventually will affect everyone around us and become a positive energy spreading throughout the world.

If you do have limiting beliefs, you can choose to dismiss an old belief and replace it with a new one. If the old belief was: *My sister is the pretty one, and I'm the smart one,* you could choose today to replace it with: *My sister is pretty, but so am I! I am also smart, an amazing cook, and a great listener.*

It doesn't matter now what someone once said about you. What matters now is what you are going to do about your limiting beliefs. If you want to decide now to change them, then do it. Your new belief can be: *Who is he or she to say what I am? I know what I am, or what I want to be. I want to be the best I can be.*

You are deserving of the best life you can have. You are important, you are respected, and you are loved. You can change anything for a fulfilling life.

I had an old limiting belief from one comment made by a friend's mother when I was a teenager. I still remember it as clear as day; I recalled a lot of these vivid memories when I was writing this book, to explain the lessons.

A friend's mother said about me, "Donna will never hold down a job, as she bites her nails."

Well, isn't that a strange thing to say? We used to talk about it when we were teenagers, and we'd say, "Remember when Mrs. D. said you'd never keep a job because you bit your nails?" I did live up to this prediction, however, as I did bite my nails for many years, and I did change jobs often.

My point is that we do remember these seemingly harmless comments, and we often act out the exact belief that was thrust upon us.

But always remember that you can choose not to take the limiting perspectives of others into your own life.

Another poignant anecdote comes from when I first met an ex-boyfriend's mother when I was nineteen years old. I was biting my nails when I met her, and she said, "Don't you love yourself?"

I was taken aback by her comment and stammered, "Pardon?"

She went on to explain that biting my nails was a sign of not loving myself. Her message made perfect sense to me: why would I deliberately harm myself if I cared for myself? This wise woman became a very influential person in my life, as was her son, and they taught me many life-changing beliefs about positive thinking and creating what you want. I was really getting the message about my nail-biting habit, which I'm happy to report I have stopped.

I'll touch on my view on the psychological reasons for nail-biting and self-harm. What causes this behavior is varied, but I relate it to being anxious or nervous. I describe myself as being hyperactive at times, and so I think it was an outlet for my nervous energy. I also smoked cigarettes (I also quit this habit many years ago).

I am not proud of having smoked, but it shows that I am qualified to comment on the power of the mind to help you quit a bad habit.

Nail-biting, picking skin, and smoking all seem to me to be forms of self-harm, as you are really hurting yourself with these habits. I'm writing this from my own perspective as someone who did these things. I didn't feel good about myself when I was biting my nails, picking skin, or smoking. At the time I wrote this book, the subject of self-harm was current. Reports of self-harm are alarmingly on the rise, and its occurrence is most common in the teen years, mostly in girls. From what I know, it's a coping strategy for negative emotions; creating the physical pain can help ease the emotional pain. This saddens me deeply. To me, it looks like a cry for help. I want to help people who are doing this and ask them to believe that they are worthy of their best life, which includes healthy habits.

There are healthy ways to feel good.
Choose them instead.

You don't need to hurt yourself to get attention. If you need attention and love, reach out to your parents or someone else you trust and tell them you need help or that you need to be heard and seen. Someone will help you. Write to me if you want more information on stopping a harmful habit or if you don't know who to turn to.

Here is another example of how one forms beliefs, but one I reacted to rather differently.

I was in my early twenties, and I was enthusiastically job seeking. The employment agent told me that if I didn't get a secretarial qualification, I wouldn't ever get a good job. The person I spoke with was very definite in telling me that I would *never* get a good job. Communication is all about tone. I learned that tone makes up 70 percent of how a message is interpreted, with body language at 20 percent, and the content a mere 10 percent. You can hear something in a loving and caring tone and get a completely different message. It was the *way* she said it; her tone and body language asserted to me, that I had better get this qualification.

I didn't believe what she said, and I remember going straight home and telling my parents the story. I had read a few books on the power of the mind, so I chose not to agree with her. I had believed from my mentors that you didn't need a formal qualification for some jobs and certainly not for the work I was interested in. My parents agreed with me that I didn't need to do the course. They didn't like her tone, and they encouraged me to pursue my media career.

At that point in my life, I had already worked in media for a few years, had a lot of experience, and was very dedicated to this career path.

I'm all for higher education if you want it or need it for your chosen profession, or simply for your interest, but at that tender age, I opted for the experience of work instead. I didn't want to do a secretarial course. I wanted to have my own business, so I went on to do that and work for myself as a marketing and event manager. Prior to being self-employed, I had many good jobs, even without a qualification, including managing the local television station, a highlight of my career.

May I add my favorite brag story of how I traveled to London on my own when I was twenty-five? I had friends from my home town of Kalgoorlie, who met me there, but I left on my own, with $1,000 Australian dollars and the pure intent to work in advertising agencies and the BBC (British Broadcasting Corporation), even though many people said, "you can't do that." One friend observed that he'd need more than $1,000 to go to Perth (our nearest capital city), for the weekend.

I went to London on a mission and arrived at Heathrow airport, where my old mate picked me up. He was laughing at my enthusiasm. I started working in an advertising agency a week after I arrived (it took me one week to spend the $1,000, which had converted to 500 British pounds). After a few months, I secured a job at the BBC, just as I'd planned to do. My new friends from London would often ask, "How did you get that job again?" I would explain that I just knew that I was going to work there, and I sold myself well in the interview. This was before I had even done the work on beliefs, but looking back now, I can see it was all about self-belief. I believed that I would work at the BBC, even though it was a highly competitive field.

Furthermore, once I had my job in the facilities department at the BBC, I would often ask to help out in other areas, as I was interested in producing television shows. I was on a temporary working visa and wanted as much experience as I could get, and I'd tell them that. They loved my enthusiasm and so would send me to the studios to watch the programs being filmed, and I'd run into famous television stars every day.

I'd go back to my home in London, a multistory and very cramped dwelling that I shared with about twenty others, and tell the others of the celebrities I'd met. I was equally as excited about the work. I have always really enjoyed working in my media and publicity jobs. It was a very exciting experience, and it felt completely right for me to be working there, as if it was meant to be.

When you love your work, life is happier. I urge you to follow your heart to do the work you love. I want you to believe that you can love your work. I tell my boys, and my readers, that you can have anything you want. When you love your work, you can work passionately, and it's fulfilling. If you are watching the clock for when it's time to finish, it's time to move on to do what you want to do. You will spend a lot of time at work, so do what you love, and this good feeling will positively affect other areas of your life.

I often say things are meant to be, and by this, I am expressing my belief that some things (jobs, people, experiences) are destined for us and that when we follow our true paths or when things come easily to us, that's when we know we're on the right path.

> ### *Life is easier when we follow our hearts, and our destinies.*

I have thought back to many experiences that I forced, and they didn't end well. When something is right for us, we don't need to force it. This goes for seeking material items, jobs, and relationships.

I have set many goals and intentions throughout my life that seemed too ambitious to others, such as publishing this book. My advice is to not listen to the naysayers and believe that you can do anything.

I have often thought back to that moment when I was told I couldn't have the big career without the secretarial qualification, and I feel good about how I trusted my own instincts.

> ### *You know what is best for you.*

So, in stark contrast to my nail-biting story from adolescence, once I had developed a mindset of choosing not to believe that what others told me was my fate but to instead create my own, I could then decide what I wanted to believe—not what others said was so.

Don't let others tell you what you can't do, can't have, or won't do. What they want for you is often not your desire anyway. Share your desires with those who will encourage and support you.

If you didn't have a supportive upbringing, you can start remedying that right away by believing what it is you want to be and how you want to be treated from now on. You don't even need to tell others around you that you are now asserting yourself. You can just decide to be treated differently. Your new decision will create a new energy around you, so you will attract different circumstances into your life. You will then behave differently, due to your new thinking.

Any situation will change once you change your thinking, change what you want, and change what you are willing to accept. It's amazing how dramatic the results can be.

Decide now that you will change your limiting beliefs into positive beliefs that make you feel good.

Notes

CHAPTER SEVEN

Let Go of the Need for Approval

Start now by making the decision that you want to love yourself, regardless of the messages you have received. You know yourself better than anyone, and you know who you are and what you want to be.

Decide not to let others determine your self-worth. You know you are a good person. You know your amazing qualities.

Focus on loving yourself, agree to love and accept yourself, and decide to love others. You don't need to rely on the approval of others to love yourself. And when you do truly love yourself, you will attract lovely people. Letting go of the need for approval from others is a very powerful change.

I believe that we seek approval from our parents, teachers, friends, partners, and many others throughout our lives.

Although we look to others for approval as we are developing our identities, we can let this need for approval go. It is very empowering to not need anyone's approval. I always felt that I had the approval of my mum and dad, and that I always had their total support. It is a wonderful feeling to still have this but not to need it.

You may not agree with everything your loved ones do, but let them be who they want to be.

Say to yourself, *I now let go of the need for approval, from anyone.* Include any people in your affirmation that you have particularly sought approval from. For example, say, *I now let go of the need for approval from Dad.* We'll pick on dads here, as it is very common to feel the need for approval from our parents. The relationships we have with our parents, caregivers, or the main people in our lives inevitably affect our feelings of self-worth.

I urge you to be around the people who are kind, loving, and supportive—the ones you feel good around. Limit the time you spend with those who do not fit this definition, or simply move away from them. When you decide that you are worthy of love and kindness, I believe that the unsuitable people will naturally move out of your life. If it is a family member or partner you are having issues with, often the situation will change when that person picks up on your new evaluation of your own self-worth.

All change in your life begins when you change. You change, and everything around you seems to change. It does change your circumstances, because you feel different, so you then attract different circumstances and different people. You cannot change others; you can only change yourself. It's amazing to experience life when you change yourself—and it all starts with how you think. Others around you will treat you differently, or they will go away if they no longer have a place in your life.

Look after yourself. Love yourself. Approve of yourself. Do what it takes to feel good now.

> ***You won't always have the approval of everyone, so approve of yourself.***

Let go of the need for approval from others, and you will feel more relaxed and feel a sense of empowerment.

Notes

CHAPTER EIGHT

Forgive Others and Forgive Yourself

With the process of loving yourself, it's important to forgive others. Forgive those who said unkind things to you. Forgive those who did unloving actions toward you. Forgive those who hurt you in any way. Say, *I forgive you (and their names).* Really feel forgiveness. You can then let go of whatever those people did or said to you and release your negative feelings.

If you find yourself thinking for any period of time about an unpleasant memory, try the following exercise. While remembering the unpleasant memory, say, *I forgive you ...* (say the person's name aloud). You can back this up with a physical action, such as brushing them off you or even lovingly sending them on their way. A ritual of this type can really help you rid yourself of the unpleasant memories. Make it as big a ritual as you need to, to let it go.

I'm all for making a big production of this ritual; you could use candles, music, whatever it takes. You can also do this to attract something into your life. There is a method or ritual perfect for you if you want to do it this way. Others may prefer to just say, *I'm over it*, and, as simple as that, the memory is gone. There are many ways to let go of past hurt, and you may also choose counseling. I strongly encourage talking to anyone you feel comfortable talking to and letting out all the emotions. Do whatever it takes for you to get past it, and do it now.

> **If you are feeling and acting as a victim, stop looking for someone to blame. Take responsibility for your own life.**

We have to take responsibility for our own lives. Think of it like this: each person has unique circumstances, and each can choose what to make of those circumstances and how to create good circumstances.

I want you to also forgive yourself. Forgive all the people you need to forgive to get on with a happy life, and forgive yourself. If you're thinking that you want to be a better parent, friend, or partner, forgive yourself.

> **We can't change our pasts, but we can affect our futures.**

We can change how we feel about what happened in the past or how we interpreted it. We can choose not to attach any meaning to an incident, or we can decide to make up a new meaning. We can decide to only remember pleasant memories. We can't control everything, but we can certainly control our own temperaments, we can choose who we spend time with, and we can choose to be optimistic, positive, and loving. Ultimately, the emotions and feelings we choose determine our actions. I believe that this is in our control.

If you feel that your own personality or mood is not up to you, and you want it to be; then consider this idea from my *Feel Good Now* book. It has been proven by neuroscientists that you can change your brain. It has been proven that you can acquire any talent or skill by practice. It is up to you. You can decide to make any change for self-improvement and a more fulfilling life. It is common for people to say, "Well, that's just me," or "That's his personality," or "I'm just like that."

You can change if you want to. If you haven't been at your best, you can change in any given moment.

Use this book as a catalyst for change. I urge you to make the changes you need to feel good for yourself and all those around you.

I've heard it said that depression is anger without enthusiasm. If you feel depressed, hopeless, or unmotivated, who are you angry at? Get these feelings out, express and release them; it could be just what you need to start feeling good now. Really get it off your chest, too. Shout, swear, hit a pillow if you need to. I believe in getting anger out by hitting a pillow; better this to release these feelings than by physically hurting someone else or yelling hurtful messages to innocent family members who will then "wear" your anger.

Talk to a friend or partner, if you choose to, about whom you want to forgive and why. You don't need to talk specifically to the person you are angry at, but it could help you to talk about your problem with someone else whom you trust. You could discover that, just by talking or thinking about this issue of forgiveness, you do have a negative belief about yourself (one that doesn't serve you), and that it was created by someone else's comments or actions. I often have those *aha* moments, where I will realize, *oh, I remember now, she said that, and I do this.* Sometimes you can see it so clearly. You can see this in other people. Use this wisdom to help yourself.

Forgiving others and yourself is a very powerful decision to make. It's an ongoing process, as I'm sure there are people we all need to forgive to be able to move on. I also believe that we don't need to go back to having a relationship or friendship with the people we want to forgive. We can forgive them and still not want them in our lives any more.

Forgive them and let them go, along with the negative emotions.

Forgiving people and deciding to let go of the negative emotions attached to them can lift a great weight off your shoulders.

There are so many better feelings to choose rather than bitterness, disappointment, and dislike. Choose to forgive yourself and others, and use that renewed energy on other, more empowering feelings.

Be loving and kind to the people who sent you the negative messages. Often people feel that the ones who "wronged" them are to blame and meant to hurt them. Choose to think instead that they did not intend to harm you or scar you emotionally. Of course there is always the possibility that you interpreted messages as you saw them, not necessarily as the other person intended. You can go further than that and believe that the person who hurt you had also been hurt by another, and so the pattern continues. Usually, people are just copying what they have seen from others; it's what they know or believe is right.

You can break this pattern by changing it.

After I did my own suggested forgiveness exercise of saying, *I forgive you …* to a friend I wanted to forgive, that night, I dreamed she visited me and apologized for her actions.

I recalled the dream vividly the next morning and remembered how she sincerely wanted my forgiveness. It was then easy to let go of this unpleasant memory. You can create your own "dream" by visualizing saying "I forgive you," or the person saying "I forgive you" to you. It is very freeing. You really will feel lighter, as though a weight has been lifted.

Playing the victim (blaming others for your life or circumstances) is a very powerless emotion. If you choose instead to believe that you control your emotions and your circumstances, that empowers you to be able to change anything. That's a much better feeling. Forgive them and love them anyway, regardless of what was said. Now create a new belief about the relationship that you are letting go. It could be that it taught you a valuable life lesson.

Another thing I ask you to do is to put this book down and hug yourself. Yes, hug yourself. You can do this. It feels good to hug yourself. If you did your naked exam (good for you!), then you can surely hug yourself.

After reading this book, I want you to love yourself or be on your way to loving yourself. If you have a loved one near you now, please hug him or her too, and say, "I love you."

Life is better when you love yourself.

Notes

Donna Hanks

Your "Love Yourself" Task

I believe that affirmations are very effective at reprogramming your mind. Here are my suggestions. You can add your own. Keep saying them until you believe them. Always use positive words in the present tense.

Write each one on the space provided and read it aloud, feeling very confident.

I love myself.

I accept myself.

I approve of myself.

I love my nose/legs/body/skin/hair (fill in your own words).

If you have someone to forgive, write this now, filling in the person's name:

I now forgive you …

If you want to let go of the need for approval, write this now, filling in the person's name:

I now let go of the need for approval from …

AFFIRMATIONS

If you want some more ideas for affirmations, here are my suggestions. Change to suit yourself.

I love myself.

I am lovable.

I am loving.

I am healthy.

I eat healthy foods.

I exercise daily.

I am beautiful.

I am fit.

I am happy.

I am a good person.

I am kind to myself and others.

I am good to myself and others.

I am loving to myself and others.

I respect myself and others.

I care for myself and others.

I approve of myself and others.

I can be, do, and have what I want.

I am grateful for all the good in my life.

I am loving my life.

I am ...

LOVE AND APPRECIATE YOURSELF

Draw a self-portrait here, or paste a favorite photo of yourself.

Write your *I am* statements around yourself.

Use this page to love and appreciate yourself.

Affirmations for Children

If you have children, please read these affirmations to them.
The children can also read them aloud.

I am lovable.

I am loving.

I am kind.

I am clever.

I am well-behaved.

I am safe at all times.

I am around loving people.

I respect others, and I respect myself.

I am beautiful in every way.

I am happy and healthy.

I am loving my life.

Write your own here:

My Vow

As an extra incentive to making your positive changes, you can choose to make your own vow.

I have written my own here. You can use this as a template for your own changes or alter the words in any way to suit yourself. Read your vow aloud, believe it, and mean it.

I vow to love myself and my children, partner, friends, and family with all my heart.

I vow to allow myself to be who I want to be.

I vow to look after myself and respect myself.

I vow to be the best I can be.

I vow to be the best parent I can be.

I vow to love my children and allow them to be who they want to be.

I vow to love my partner and allow him to be who he wants to be.

I vow to love my friends and family and allow them to be who they want to be.

I vow to be kind and loving to all and think good thoughts.

I vow to encourage others to be the best they can be.

I vow to forgive everyone.

I vow to forgive myself.

I vow to release the need for approval from anyone.

I vow to let it all go.

You can cut this affirmation out and stick it on your fridge, mirror, desk, or anywhere you like. It reminds you to love yourself.

If you have children, please also put this message on their bathroom mirror, or where they will read it every day.

(You can also write it on a mirror with erasable pens designed for writing on glass).

I
love
you

Thank you

I trust that you enjoyed reading *I Love You*.

Thank you to everyone who has supported me while writing this book and presenting my seminars.

Thank you and I love you Dean, James, and Jack. Words can't express my love for you. I love you more than there is a word for and I love you 100 percent.

To Mum, Dad, Steve, and Scott—thank you for being my loving family and for all your support and love.

To my family and friends, who have listened to my coaching, and have coached me when I needed it. If you're mentioned in this book, you've had a dramatic influence in my life, and I thank you for that.

Special mention to Niki, Julie, and Jenny; thank you for the life lessons and your constant support and love.

Thank you, Donna C., for being the first person to read this and tell me you loved it. Your praise touched me.

I especially want to thank and recommend my mentor, Siimon Reynolds. Siimon is an Australian advertising and business expert, now based in Los Angeles. He is a brilliant business coach, author of numerous bestselling books, and founder of a half-billion-dollar company. I have learned many valuable lessons from his books and business coaching, and he has supported my many ventures. He has always encouraged me to keep going. Siimon believes that persistence is the number-one element, key to achieving your desires. I highly recommend Siimon as an exceptional business coach and speaker. Visit www.siimonreynolds.com for more information.

Thank you to all my self-development teachers, who have all contributed to my knowledge and theories.

My last thank you is to you, my reader. Thank you for reading my book. I would love to hear your feedback and your own success stories.

www.donnahanks.com

Printed in Australia
AUOC02n2215131215
272428AU00002B/2/P

9 781452 531755